Maple trees in bright fall colors

Fall

Mary L. Meyer

A⁺
Smart Apple Media

COPYRIGHT

🍂 Published by Smart Apple Media

1980 Lookout Drive, North Mankato, MN 56003

Designed by Rita Marshall

Copyright © 2003 Smart Apple Media. International copyright reserved in all countries. No part of this book may be reproduced in any form without written permission from the publisher.

Printed in the United States of America

🍂 Photographs by Dennis Frates, Paul T. McMahon, Tom Stack & Associates

(J. Lotter Gurling, Victoria Hurst, Thomas Kitchin, Spencer Swanger)

🍂 Library of Congress Cataloging-in-Publication Data

Meyer, Mary L. Fall / by Mary L. Meyer. p. cm. — (Seasons)

Includes bibliographical references and index.

Summary: Describes the climate and activities of autumn and the ways in which some animals and plants prepare for the colder days ahead.

🍂 ISBN 1-58340-141-5

1. Autumn—Juvenile literature. [1. Autumn.] I. Title.

QB637.7 .M49 2002   508.2—dc21   2001049974

🍂 First Edition 9 8 7 6 5 4 3 2 1

Fall Weather

Cold, frosty nights and shorter days are signs that summer has ended and winter is coming. In northern regions, such as the United States and Canada, the first day of fall is September 22 or 23. Fall is so named because it is a time of falling leaves. Some people also call this season "autumn."

The seasons change because the earth is tipped on its **axis** as it travels around the sun. In the fall, the northern half of the earth begins to point away from the sun. The days often stay

Fallen leaves decorate the banks of a creek

warm, but the nights become chilly. If the ground cools quickly at night, tiny droplets of water called dew form on grass and other objects. Dew does not come from clouds; it comes from the air. During the day, the sun's heat causes the water in the ground to **evaporate**. When the sun sets, the ground cools, and the water in the air **condenses**. Fall

A hurricane has a center, or "eye," that is calm, with no wind and clear, blue sky.

can be a time of severe storms. It marks the start of hurricane season. Hurricanes are spinning storms with strong winds and heavy rain that occur in the Atlantic Ocean. During the fall, just

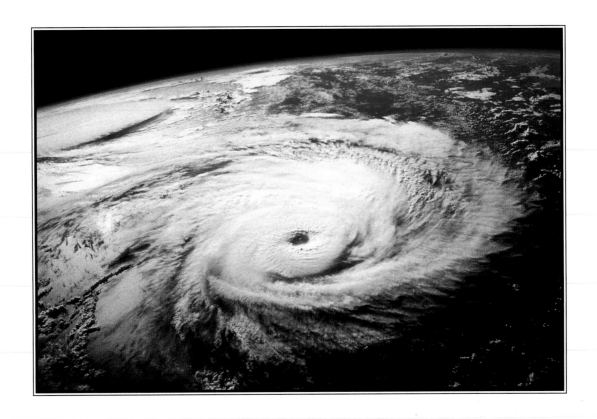

about any kind of weather is possible. For example, on November 11, 1911, the temperature in Kansas City, Missouri, was 76 °F (24 °C) in the morning, and in the afternoon, snow fell.

Bales of hay wait for the final harvest

Stocking Up

Many animals store food for winter during the fall. Animals such as squirrels and chipmunks bury nuts and seeds in the ground. Honeybees store honey in their hives. Acorn woodpeckers make holes in tree trunks and poke acorns into them. Some animals eat large amounts of food to fatten themselves up, then find a place to **hibernate**. Small, mouse-like creatures hibernate in hollow logs or underground. Hibernating bats may choose barns,

In addition to storing fruits and nuts, some animals store dry leaves underground to eat during the winter.

attics, or caves. Hibernating animals lower their body temper-

ature to save energy. Raccoons and bears do not truly hiber-

nate, but they may sleep in their dens for many days at a time.

Squirrels spend the fall collecting food for the winter

Many birds migrate to warmer places in the fall. They do not migrate because the weather is cold, but because insects and green plants are scarce. In Canada and the United States, flocks of geese travel hundreds of miles to the south where food is plentiful. When the temperature becomes colder, some insects migrate

Each fall, monarch butterflies migrate from Canada to Mexico, a distance of 1,240 miles (2,012 km).

south to warmer areas. Others lay eggs that will hatch in the spring. But many insects die.

A mallard duck takes off on its way south

Changing Leaves

Leafy trees undergo a big change in the fall. A special layer of **cells** forms on each leaf. This layer blocks the flow of water into the leaves. The green food-making cells in the leaves die without water. When the green cells die, cells of other colors appear—beautiful shades of red, orange, and yellow. Maple trees are some of the most colorful fall trees.

Many plants bear fruit that ripens in the fall. Examples include apples, pumpkins, and corn. As animals eat the fruit, the seeds

Leaves make colorful patterns when they fall

inside fall to the ground and settle in the soil. Seeds are also scattered by the wind or carried on the fur of animals to new places. These seeds will not start to grow right away. If they did, the young plants would freeze and die. The seeds "sleep" until warm temperatures and spring rains awaken them. Although some plants die in the fall, the roots of other plants stay alive underground through the winter and start to grow again in the spring.

Birds help to scatter seeds by eating berries. The undigested seeds pass through the bird and are left in its droppings.

Fall Activities

Many farmers harvest their crops in the fall.

Around the world, people celebrate the harvest by sharing in

A farmer harvests a field of grain

large feasts and giving thanks for good fortune and good health. In North America, many families gather for Thanksgiving. *Chu Sok* is the harvest festival in Korea. Jewish families celebrate *Sukkoth*. Fall is a time of much change and activity for plants and animals. Every living thing must get ready for the less bountiful months ahead. People harvest crops, go back to school, and enjoy the colorful leaves before the winter snow returns.

The harvest moon was so named because it shines so brightly that farmers can work late at night harvesting their crops.

More fall sunlight makes trees turn a brighter red

Seedy Snack

Roasted pumpkin seeds make a tasty, healthy snack. Pumpkins are bountiful in the fall, and their seeds are easy to prepare. (Ask an adult for help with this activity.)

What You Need

Seeds from a large pumpkin
Water
Measuring spoons
A mixing spoon

A cookie sheet
Vegetable oil
A mixing bowl
An oven

What You Do

1. Rinse the pumpkin seeds with water to clean them.
2. Have an adult help you preheat the oven to 250 °F (120 °C).
3. Mix two tablespoons (30 ml) of vegetable oil with the seeds in the mixing bowl.
4. Spread the seeds on the cookie sheet and bake for 30 minutes.
5. Allow the seeds to cool completely and enjoy!

Pumpkins ripen in October, in time for Halloween

INFORMATION

Index

Words to Know

axis (AK-sis)—the imaginary line through the earth that connects the North and South Poles

cells (SELLZ)—the tiny building blocks of all plant and animal life

condenses (con-DEN-sez)—changes from a gas to a liquid

evaporate (ee-VAP-uh-rate)—to change from a liquid to a gas

hibernate (HI-burr-nayt)—to spend the winter in a resting state

migrate (MY-grate)—to move from one area to another according to the changing seasons

Read More

Baxter, Nicola. *Autumn*. Danbury, Conn.: Children's Press, 1996.

Robbins, Ken. *Autumn Leaves*. New York: Scholastic Press, 1998.

Stone, Lynn M. *Autumn As the Earth Turns*. Vero Beach, Fla.: The Rourke Book Co., 1994.

Internet Sites

FEMA for Kids: Hurricanes
http://www.fema.gov/kids/hurr.htm

University of Illinois Extension: The Miracle of Fall
http://www.urbanext.uiuc.edu/fallcolor

Monarch Watch
http://www.MonarchWatch.org/